Model Yachts And Model Yacht Sailing

MODEL YACHTS AND MODEL YACHT SAILING.

BOOKS OF INSTRUCTION AND AMUSEMENT.

THE BOY'S OWN TOY MAKER:

A Practical Illustrated Guide to the useful employment of Leisure Hours. By E. LANDELS. With 200 Cuts. Ninth Edition. Price 2s. 6d.

"A new and valuable form of endless amusement."—*Nonconformist.*

"We recommend it to all who have children to be instructed and amused."
—*Economist.*

THE GIRL'S OWN TOY MAKER

AND BOOK OF RECREATION.

By E. and A. LANDELS. With 200 Illustrations. New Edition. The Eleventh Thousand. Just ready. Price 2s. 6d.

"Contains a large number of engravings, and gives instruction, with many examples, how to make Paper Toys, &c., &c., in which young people especially take interest."—*Leeds Mercury.*

"Within the past few years great advancement has been made in the educational system it is meant to encourage, and it is, therefore, all the more likely to obtain a still wider circulation."—*Edinburgh Daily Review.*

"Capital little volume . . . will be found a rare prize for families."—*City Press.*

"We can easily imagine the delight with which a family of children would welcome this interesting work."—*Scholastic World.*

THE ILLUSTRATED
PAPER MODEL MAKER;

Containing Twelve Subjects and Practical Diagrams for their Construction, in an Envelope. Price 2s.

GRIFFITH & FARRAN,
WEST CORNER OF ST. PAUL'S CHURCHYARD, LONDON.

E. P. DUTTON & CO., NEW YORK.

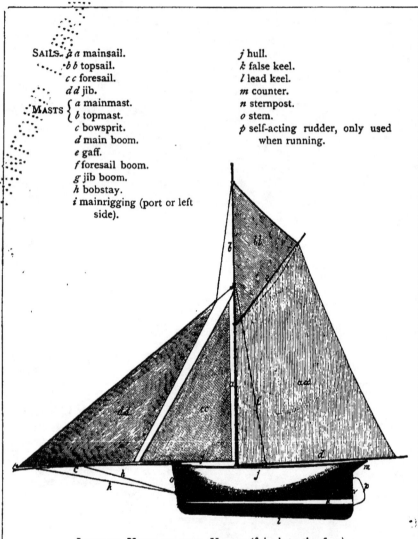

SAILS. *a a* mainsail.
b b topsail.
c c foresail.
d d jib.

MASTS { *a* mainmast.
b topmast.
c bowsprit.
d main boom.
e gaff.
f foresail boom.
g jib boom.
h bobstay.
i mainrigging (port or left side).

j hull.
k false keel.
l lead keel.
m counter.
n sternpost.
o stem.
p self-acting rudder, only used when running.

LATERAL VIEW OF 3-FT. YACHT (⅔ inch to the foot).
For deck outline and measurement of this Model "Diana" Cutter, see diagram 8, p. 19.

A SELF...

ILLUSTRATED...

GRIFFITH...

MDCCCLXXX

MODEL YACHTS
AND MODEL YACHT SAILING.

HOW TO BUILD, RIG, AND SAIL

A SELF-ACTING MODEL YACHT.

BY

JAMES E. WALTON, V.M.Y.C.

ILLUSTRATED WITH FIFTY-EIGHT ENGRAVINGS.

GRIFFITH AND FARRAN,
SUCCESSORS TO NEWBERY AND HARRIS,
WEST CORNER OF ST. PAUL'S CHURCHYARD, LONDON.
E. P. DUTTON AND CO., NEW YORK.
MDCCCLXXX.

193292

[*The rights of Translation and of Reproduction are reserved.*]

CONTENTS.

	PAGE
PREFACE	11
INTRODUCTION	15
CHAP. I. PRINCIPLES OF SELF-ACTING MODEL YACHT BUILDING	21
,, II. HOW TO MAKE THE HULL	31
,, III. HOW TO MAKE DECK FITTINGS, RUDDER, &c.	47
,, IV. HOW TO FIT MASTS, STANDING AND RUNNING GEAR, &c.	57
,, V. HOW TO MAKE THE SAILS AND SET THEM	73
,, VI. HOW TO SAIL AND STEER A MODEL YACHT	85
MATERIALS FOR MODEL SHIPS	97
GLOSSARY	100
MODEL YACHT CONTESTS ON THE SEA	102
TABLES OF MODEL YACHT REGATTAS	103
WATERS IN LONDON FOR MODEL YACHT SAILING	104

PREFACE

There are not many open-air amusements which afford more genuine enjoyment to old and young than Model Yacht Sailing; if practised in a properly scientific manner it resembles a game of croquet, in which the water is the lawn, the wind the mallet, and the ships the balls; and the most skilful yachtsman is as certain of winning his match as is the most skilful croquet player.

Very few English boys can be found who have not taken, or do not take an interest in model ships, and it is very remarkable, as well as no little disgrace to us as a maritime nation, to note the utterly purposeless way in which nearly all boys or men sail their model vessels; whereas with the requisite knowledge, a self-acting model yacht is as much under the control of the manager as if he were actually on board: further still, matches can be sailed in which the results are as certain as are those of the matches of ordinary yachts, as may be seen in the tables of actual races at the end of this work (see p. 103).

A sailor who thoroughly understands the management of a ship or boat, *when he is on board, steers with a rudder*, and *reduces, augments*, or *disposes* the sails at his will, would find this knowledge of very secondary importance if he applied it, *without great modifications*, to sail a model yacht. To give one instance only, *model yachts require no fixed rudder*, in fact, a fixed rudder is such an incumbrance, and so great a bar to perfect action, that it must be dispensed with altogether. This quite upsets the old adage of a "ship without a rudder," and reverses it; our model ships need no rudder—steer better without, save in one way.

A rudder is used at times on model yachts, as will be shown in its place, but it must be removed when it has done its work.

The sails and hulls of model yachts are also very different to those of full-sized yachts. They are constructed with the *view to being self-acting*, and as a model yacht *must steer itself*, this result can only be obtained by using the sails both for *propelling and steering*.

Model yachts, as usually made, may be very beautiful to look at, but, alas! they will not sail, or will not sail well, they are not self-acting in any sense, they are generally actual reproductions in miniature of celebrated large yachts, and as these latter are sailed and steered by men on board, it is very certain their miniature copies will not sail without similar guidance.

I have made these remarks to show that model self-acting yachts cannot be made and sailed without the requisite knowledge and experience, and as there is no book to be got which gives full particulars on the subject, it is believed that this, which contains the result of many years' model yacht making and sailing, will supply an almost national want, and enable any ordinarily intelligent boy to construct, rig, and sail a model yacht with perfect success.

As a proof of the pains that have been taken to ascertain the best hull and rig for a self-acting yacht, I may say that five yachts have been made, all of the same length, but each of different beam, rig, &c., commencing with very narrow beam, and increasing beam, &c., with each model, till the best proportion between length and beam became known,—necessarily with each increase of beam *more sail could be carried*, and also more *ballast in lead keel* could be used,—and in order that the experiments should be crucial and decisive, a final vessel was constructed of the same measurement as the best of those before mentioned, and their sails were made interchangeable, thus deciding beyond doubt which vessel was best, after many trials on the open sea with a true wind.

It is doubtful if such experiments were ever made before (tables of them will be seen at p. 102), and the author, therefore, feels assured that his readers may have every confidence in the instruction here given.

INTRODUCTION.

THE first thing necessary for non-nautical yachtsmen is to know the names of the different sails, parts of the vessel, &c., &c., and for this purpose the diagram forming the frontispiece will be useful; a glossary, also, is added at the end of the work.

The frontispiece is an exact outline drawing of a model self-acting yacht, of 3-feet water-line, and 39 in. over all; the diagram is drawn in the proportion of ⅜ in. to the foot, and if any reader desires to make a smaller boat, say 30 in., all that need be done is to make everything ¼ smaller, and for a 2-ft. boat ⅓ smaller; as the keel, however, would have to be calculated by weight, and the above rule would not apply, I give the weight in lbs.; a 3-ft. boat requires

20 lbs., a 2-ft.-6-in. boat 10 or 11 lbs., and a 24-in. boat 6 lbs. or nearly.

I will note here that it is better to make a vessel scooped out, &c., from the solid block, than to build one of small planks; 1st, it is easier (it takes a good carpenter to make one of planks), it can be altered outside if not scooped out too thin at first, it never *leaks*, and it never comes to pieces; and, lastly, it does not take half the time to repaint, &c., &c.

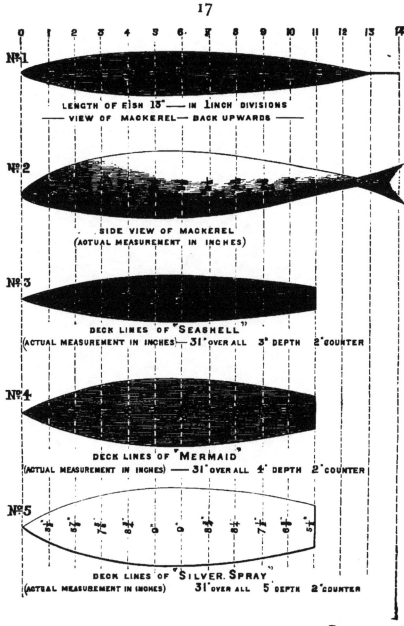

19

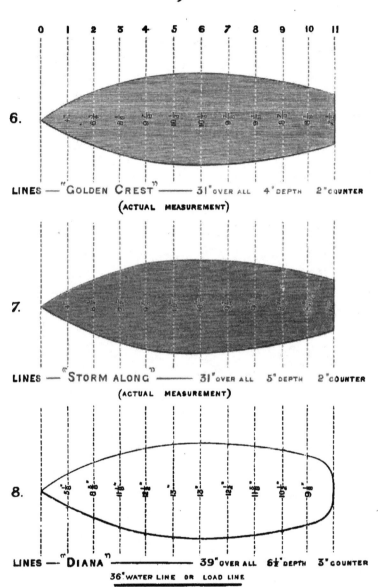

6.

LINES — "GOLDEN CREST" ——— 31" OVER ALL   4" DEPTH   2" COUNTER
(ACTUAL MEASUREMENT)

7.

LINES — "STORM ALONG" ——— 31" OVER ALL   5" DEPTH   2" COUNTER
(ACTUAL MEASUREMENT)

8.

LINES — "DIANA" ——————— 39" OVER ALL   6½" DEPTH   3" COUNTER
36" WATER LINE OR LOAD LINE

B 2

CHAPTER I.

PRINCIPLES OF MODEL YACHT BUILDING.

CHAPTER I.

PRINCIPLES OF MODEL YACHT BUILDING.

IN order to ascertain the best lines, *i.e.* shape, for progression through the water, Nature herself may, without hesitation, be taken as the best teacher, and amongst fast-moving fishes a mackerel is one of the fastest and most graceful.

I procured a mackerel, carefully measured and drew it to scale (see p. 17, diagrams 1 and 2), first taking the shape back upwards, and next sideways, and in harmony with these lines all the vessels mentioned in this work are constructed.

On looking at the diagram of the mackerel it is at once apparent that a clean run is more important than a sharp entrance, for the drawing shows the fish to be much fuller in the fore than in the after part; bearing this in mind, and having drawn the mackerel in divisions of inches, I took the forward eleven divisions as a model for the deck and general lines of my vessels —first, so far as regards "*going through the water;*" secondly, because I should thus get "*the widest part or beam amidships*," and as near the centre of motion and gravity as possible.

With these ideas in my mind I constructed "Seashell" (see diagram 3, p. 17), with the actual measurements there stated (as is the case on all the drawings). I rigged her as a schooner; thus—

She sailed well and steadily, and could be made to go in any direction in a light breeze, but her *narrow beam*

and lightness, with only 3 lbs. keel, rendered her useless in a stiff breeze, except when she was running away from it.

I next built "Mermaid" (see diagram 4), with nearly 2 in. more beam, and exactly to the measurement of the mackerel sideways, simply increasing each line in proportion as the ship was larger than the fish; all the lines of the hull being of course in harmony with the increased beam, she had 5 lbs. lead keel, and was rigged as a cutter (see "Diana" for cutter rig, frontispiece), schooner, or lugger at pleasure. I found she beat "Seashell" considerably in any wind, but especially in strong winds, sailing under any of the above-mentioned sails.

Learning by this that increased beam and weight meant more power, more sail, and greater speed, I then made "Silver Spray" (see diagram 5), with 8 lbs. keel, and nearly 2 in. more beam than "Mermaid," and in this vessel I reached about the proportional beam that most model yacht builders have adopted, viz. 3½ beams to the length. I rigged her as a cutter only, and she easily beat "Mermaid" every way. I also discovered that cutter rig was best, the boats under this rig sailing faster and truer, and are more quickly and expeditiously managed; at the same time I discarded fixed rudders for reasons stated before.

With this model, "Silver Spray," I had reached a point at which I stuck for some time; I could hardly think still increased beam or depth would be an advantage, yet I wished to progress, and try something I would.

I thought the matter over carefully, and at last arrived at the following conclusions: A fish goes *through the water only, but a ship goes through and over.* Now a duck goes over the water; how would a vessel built upon a combination of fish and duck succeed?

I got a duck, took a plaster cast of his under side, noticed the way ducks got over the water, the resistance of the water and the ripples and wake caused by the duck's motion over the water, and I decided to make a ship to go *over the water rather than through it;* the top of the *water is alive*, and easily displaced in any direction save downwards, the deeper one goes the stiller it is, and the more difficult to displace. I considered, therefore, if I built a vessel of greater beam, very light draught of water, with a lead keel well below the bottom, I should get greatly increased power and speed, for I felt satisfied that the light draught and larger sails more than compensated for a wider beam.

It stands also to reason that a vessel of a wide beam does *not heel over to leeward* so much as one of a narrower beam, and it results from that—1st, the sails being more perpendicular to the wind, have more power to propel; and 2nd, the keel being also more "up and down," prevents her making so much leeway.

No doubt there is a limit to breadth of beam, and although I have not yet fully experimented, I am inclined to think that the limit is reached in "Diana," of three beams to the length.

On this I built "Golden Crest" (see diagram 6, p. 19), with these qualities, beam 10⅓ in., or ⅓ her length exactly, and only a bare 4 in. depth, and 10 lbs. lead keel; I fitted her with sails as a cutter, making them larger than those of "Silver Spray," in proportion to her increased beam and ballast (in lead keel), and she more than fulfilled my utmost expectations, for she beat all the three former models out and out, both in speed and steadiness.

Still, however, I had not quite finished my experiments, for I remarked that in strong winds "Golden Crest," on account of her low freeboard (*i.e.* little height out of the water), was sometimes overpowered sooner than I thought she ought to be, and I determined to build another vessel on the same lines and of the same size exactly, but with 1 in. deeper hold; this I did in "Storm Along" (see diagram 7, p. 19), the only difference between this and "Golden Crest" being the 1 in. extra depth of hold; lead keel, sails, masts, &c., &c., all were exactly the same.

Now, when Greek meets Greek, then comes the tug of war. So it was here, and it was only after numberless trials in all winds, and finally by actually interchanging their sails, that "Storm Along" proved the winner; the reason this was difficult to establish was that at first I only sailed *each with its own sails;* when the wind was moderate and sea smooth, "Golden Crest" won a little; on the other hand, with strong breezes and sea on, "Storm Along" won. I interchanged their sails, and "Storm Along" won considerably always. I then found out that I had happened to lace the feet of the sails of "Storm Along" to their booms, but it never struck me such a trifle would interfere much with the sailing of a model: I was mistaken, however, for I found whichever had the laced sails was sure to lose, and "Golden Crest" lost most; mind, all these experiments were conducted on the open sea for hours, with true winds and true sea (the most perfect test). I cut the sails loose, and at once and ever after, "Storm Along" proved invariably the victor; in light winds by very, very little, but in strong winds the greater buoyancy, and therefore lateral power, of "Storm Along" always carried the day.

With all these ships there are *no bulwarks*, no ornaments, or projections of any kind, nothing but the gear, &c., necessary to set the sails and work them; everything else is not only useless, but mischievous lumber.

It may be remarked that the whole of those boats when running before the wind, with self-acting lead rudders, run at very nearly the *same speed*, length to a great extent governing speed; but on turning to windward, each falls into its place, as assigned to it in the foregoing pages.

I have not yet tried whether greater beam still than ⅓ the length is an improvement; I am resting on my oars awhile, and perhaps some one else may undertake the experiment.

Particulars of the races between "Golden Crest" and "Storm Along" are noted on p. 102.

CHAPTER II.

HOW TO MAKE THE HULL.

CHAPTER II.

HOW TO MAKE THE HULL.

BEFORE entering upon the subject of this chapter, I will enumerate the tools which will be needed : these are a small axe, saw, plane, 1-in. gouge, ½-in. gouge, a rasp, a bradawl, a screw-driver, a gimlet, a hammer, a pair of small round-nosed pliers, a rat-tail file, a half-round file, a small mallet, and last, though not least, a good pocket-knife.

It is best and easiest, at any rate for beginners, to cut out model ships from a solid block, because if not scooped out too thin, alterations can be made on the outside if desirable; if the block, in process of cutting out, should split, rub it with a piece of flannel dipped in linseed oil every time after working on it, the tools cut just as easily, and all liability to split is obviated.

To make a 3-ft. yacht (see lateral view, frontispiece;

deck outline, diagram 8, p. 19; and sectional outlines, p. 37), get a block of deal, with as few knots and cracks in it as possible, and well-seasoned; it must be 39 in. long, 13 in. wide, and 8 in. deep; thus—

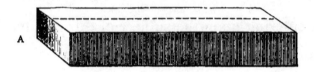

Divide it into two exact halves, as shown by the dotted line—this centre line must *never be lost* or *rubbed out till the hull is finished;* choose the best side for the deck or upper side, divide it lengthways into eleven compartments or divisions, and carefully set off on each side the length of each line (as shown in diagram 8, p. 19); thus—

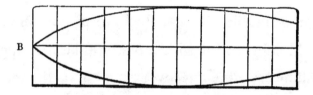

With the axe (mind all the tools are sharp) chop off carefully both sides of the block till it is shaped thus—

How to Make the Hull.

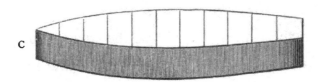

With the gouge cut out the run and entrance in the bottom of the piece of wood, beginning a little forward of the middle for the run; and at same time cut away so much of the bottom as will leave ½ in. for the keel, by ⅝ wide. The next diagram shows one side, with entrance and run cut out.

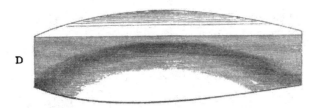

Having cut out the other side to *correspond exactly*, and rounded the sides and bottom with the plane and rasp, taking care all the curved parts are in keeping with the curves of the deck diagram C, saw a slanting piece off the cutwater, about ½ in. at bottom to nothing at top, measure 36 in. from the middle of the cutwater towards the stern, and cut out the piece of keel in the run, so as to leave the counter (projecting of the stern); thus (the dotted lines show where and how to cut)—

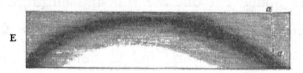

The counter must not project more than 3 in., and therefore the ship will be 3 ft. keel, and 3 ft. 3 in. over all. Now smooth and model the ship to your best ability, see the keel *is quite straight*, and the *sternpost perpendicular to the stempost or cutwater* (*a a* is the sternpost in above diagram E).

If the vessel is now exactly equal on both sides, and not lob-sided, as sailors call it, you can finish it with the rasp, scrape it with glass, and polish it with sand paper, making the outside look perfectly ship-shape.

The sectional views here shown enable the model ship builder to judge of the correctness of his work ; they represent the hull *when finished*, if cut athwart or across

How to Make the Hull.

into four pieces of equal length, and by holding the vessel in the required position the builder can see if his model present these or nearly these outlines exteriorly; if so, it is right.

It is not at all necessary to adhere exactly to this outline of the midship section (although it governs the outlines of the other two); it may be cut somewhat flatter on the bottom, as indicated by the dotted lines, and this would of course slightly vary the other sectional outlines, but I do not think it should be made more angular, nor do I advise it, as the vessel would lose too much buoyancy.

SECTIONAL VIEWS.

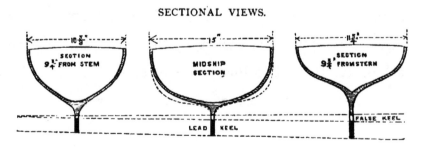

The next thing is to scoop it out with the gouge and mallet. Leave the sides everywhere ⅜ or ½ in. thick, and be careful not to scoop thinner, or leave the sides thicker in one part than another.

The gouge is the principal tool for this work, but a centrebit, to bore holes all over the inside, is a great assistance, it saves half the hammering; however, when scooped out and the inside smoothed, your vessel should look thus—

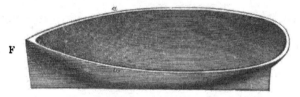

Next make the *sheer* by planing out the gunwale (gunwale *a a*), beginning at nothing forward at the stem, gradually increasing to ½ in. amidships, and again decreasing to nothing at the stern. The diagram G below shows clearly what is meant by the sheer, and how to fashion it: the dotted line is the sheer—

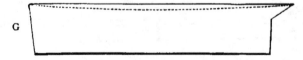

and a vessel looks very stiff and ungraceful without it.

Now give the inside a coat of white paint, and then the deck can be put on. The deck must be made of one piece of deal plank, without splits or knots, ¼ in. thick at the sides, and ⅜ in. in the middle; this gives the deck a slightly rounded appearance, and, besides, greatly strengthens it. Mark the shape of the gunwale on the plank by turning the ship bottom upwards upon it, and marking it round with a pencil; draw a middle line from end to end, and cut it to the required shape as near as possible.

A beam must now be put across the middle of the ship, exactly level with the gunwale on both sides, to support the deck and strengthen the sides of the ship; the beam should be ½ in. square; thus—

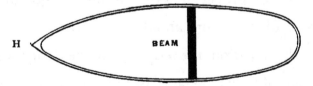

Screw the sides of the ship to the ends of the beam; then put on the deck, and screw it to the gunwale all round with ½-in. brass (everything must be brass except the lead keel) screws at about equal distances of 3 in., and two or three screws through the deck into the beam; if this is done in a workmanlike way, and the edge of the deck planed off and smoothed level with the side of the ship, the hull ought to be perfect, and practically water-tight. Mind in putting in the beam to leave place for the hatchway or step of the mast.

The next operation is to put on the keels—false and leaden. The false keel is simply a strip of beech, oak, or mahogany, of the same length as the keel of the ship, ⅜ in. thick, ½ in. deep at one end, and 1 in. at the other; thus—

This must be screwed into the keel of the ship with brass screws of proper length, *i.e.* not to go through the bottom of the ship, about 6 in. apart. This false keel, and the position it occupies, can be easily seen in the drawing of "Diana," and is marked K; the leaden keel is underneath as there shown, and I will now describe the best way to make it.

How to Make the Hull.

20 lbs. of lead will be required for a 3-ft. yacht, as before stated, and the lead can be melted in any old pot, on any ordinary clear kitchen fire. First make an oblong narrow box or mould of any smooth ½-in. boards —*dry*, or the lead will splutter and be full of air-holes —3 ft. long inside, ⅝ in. inside width, 2 in. deep at one end, and 3 in. at the other; this will hold about 20 lbs. of lead, and here follows a drawing of the mould.

Into the bottom of this mould, and sticking upright, as shown in the drawing, must be placed at equal distances six or eight pegs, beginning about 1 in. from the extreme ends of the mould; these pegs must be rather thicker than the screws intended to screw the leaden to the false keel, and will, as no doubt the intelligent reader already perceives, leave holes in the cast leaden keel for the screws to go through, these screws may be long enough to go through the false keel into the ship's bottom, and the work will be all the stronger and better. Having melted the lead, pour it at once into the mould, and the keel is made; when cool take it out of the mould, trim it, smooth the sides and top and bottom with the plane, and let the shape be something thus—

Screw it on to and through the false keel (if you cannot make holes through the false keel to receive the screws without danger of splitting it, bore them in their proper places with the bradawl, and then burn them out with a red-hot skewer); the thickest end of the keel must be aft or behind, and when screwing it on mind and bore out the top of the holes in the lead, so that the heads of the screws may be quite level with the lead (this operation is called countersinking the screws); the heaviest end of the lead is put aft so as to make the ship well up at the stem and deep at the stern;

the reason for this will be given in the chapter on "sailing a model yacht."

It may, however, be well to add here that the false keel, by holding the leaden keel at a greater distance from the bottom of the ship, greatly increases the *leverage of the leaden keel without increasing the weight*, and gives great hold upon the water, however little water the hull may draw, so that more sail can be carried, and the ship steer better with this arrangement than without it.

Now try how she floats, and if she floats about 3 in. deeper aft than forward, that will do.

Next get a strip of sheet brass about 5 ft. long, ½ in. wide, and ⅛ in. thick; most likely you will have to get this soldered in two or three pieces; it is to make a band to cover the leaden keel at the bottom, ends, and also the stem and sternpost, to keep them from being injured by stones, &c., on striking the shore, &c.; holes must be punched in it at every 3 in. where it covers the lead, and at every inch where it covers the wood of the stem and sternpost.

44   *Model Yachts and Model Yacht Sailing.*

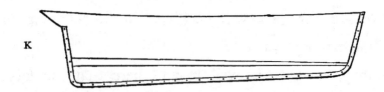

The above drawing shows what is meant, and the place it occupies (I have distorted the drawing to show it better); it must be screwed with brass ½-in. screws, countersunk, to the lead keel, &c., as above stated; the cutwater part of it must be filed away to ¼ in. wide, the rest may be left ½ in. wide. This has always been to me the most difficult operation, and it must be well done and put on perfectly straight at bottom and both ends.

When screwing it on leave one hole without screw in the stem for the bobstay, and two in the sternpost for the self-acting rudder, as shown in this drawing.

The one in the stem must be about 5 in. from top, and

How to Make the Hull. 45

the two in the sternpost about 5 in. apart—the black dots show the places.

The hull is now finished; next scratch the deck with straight lines ½ in. apart from stem to stern to imitate planks, leaving ¼ in. margin all round to look like a gunwale, and with the following remarks I will close this chapter.

It must be understood that it is almost impossible to mention every operation; many things, and the way to do them, must be left to the ingenuity and skill of the builder; it is sufficient that if my directions have been reasonably carried out, the result, so far, will be a good seaworthy model yacht's hull.

I have given in this chapter and elsewhere the dimensions for a 3-ft. boat, because it is easier to work downwards from a large size than upwards from a small one. There is less chance of mistake, for an error in a 2-ft. boat would be multiplied by working upwards, while the same error would be decreased in working downwards.

A 3-ft. boat is somewhat large and heavy; 2 ft. and

2 ft. 6 in. are the best sizes. Indeed, unless a large boat is specially required, beginners should not attempt anything larger than a 2-ft. boat, and even a boat 1 ft. 6 in. is a very good size for boys, and will sail, &c., as well as a 3-ft. boat, though of course not so fast.

I append tables of measurement for the blocks of wood and weight of keels for all these sizes:—

For 3-ft. boat, block 39" × 13" × 8", keel 20 lbs.
  „ 2-ft.-6-in. boat, „ $32\frac{1}{2}$ × $10\frac{5}{8}$ × $6\frac{3}{8}$ „   10 „
  „ 2-ft. boat,   „   26 × $8\frac{3}{8}$ × $5\frac{1}{8}$ „   7 „
  „ 1-ft.-6-in. boat, „ $19\frac{1}{2}$ × $6\frac{1}{2}$ × 4   „   3 „

It would not matter if in the large sizes the keel were a pound or so heavier, and in the small a half-pound or so; but on no account must they be lighter in any case. I also add the weight of the leaden rudders necessary to make the vessels run before the wind.

    3-ft. boat requires $1\frac{1}{4}$ lbs.
    2-ft.-6-in. boat „ $\frac{3}{4}$ „
    2-ft. boat   „ $\frac{1}{2}$ „
    1-ft.-6-in. boat „ $\frac{1}{4}$ „

For the masts, sails, and tackle of smaller boats, the calculation of size may be easily made.

CHAPTER III.

HOW TO MAKE DECK FITTINGS, RUDDER, &c.

CHAPTER III.

HOW TO MAKE DECK FITTINGS, RUDDER, ETC.

I purpose in this chapter to show how to make and fit all that is required on the deck to secure and work the rigging and sails. The following is a diagram of the deck of the ship, with each object in its proper place, and further on will be given enlarged drawings of each, with description :—

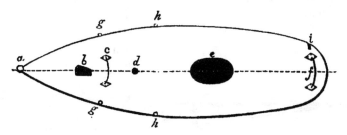

The first object, *a*, is a 1½-in. or 2-in. screw-eye, with large eye for the bowsprit to go through; this must be carefully screwed into the thick wood at the stem through the deck; *b* is the chock for the heel or inner end of the bowsprit to fit in; *c* is the horse for the foresheet to work on; *d* is the hole or step for the mainmast; *e* is the hatchway or opening in the deck, just large enough to admit the hand easily; *f* is the horse for the mainsheet to travel on; *g g* and *h h* are 1-in. eye-bolts (screw-eyes) for the bowsprit guys, and main-backstays to be hooked to; these must be firm and strong. Here is a diagram of masts, spars, and rigging only.

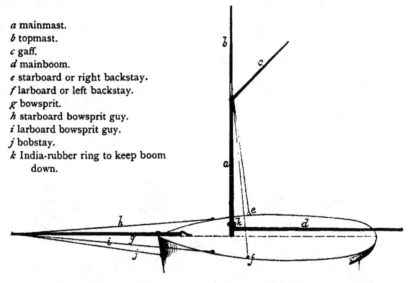

a mainmast.
b topmast.
c gaff.
d mainboom.
e starboard or right backstay.
f larboard or left backstay.
g bowsprit.
h starboard bowsprit guy.
i larboard bowsprit guy.
j bobstay.
k India-rubber ring to keep boom down.

Inserting the screw-eye for the bowsprit, *a*, requires no explanation: it must be just large enough in the eye for

How to Make Deck Fittings, Rudder, &c. 51

the bowsprit to go through; if not large enough, file it to the necessary size with the rat-tail file.

The chock *b* (p. 49) must be made out of a piece of oak or mahogany about 3 in. long, and about 1 in. thick; a hole ½ in. deep, and of the diameter of the end or heel of the bowsprit should be made in it; thus— ; the other end may be tapered off to taste, and screwed strongly right through into the deck exactly amidships. It should be of such a height that when the bowsprit is in its place it shall be perfectly in a line with the mid-deck line, and also with the stem and stern (as shown in the diagram, p. 50). The chock may be placed any distance from the stem, so long as it is not too close to the horse for foresheet (diagram, p. 49).

The horse for foresheet is made as follows: Cut two diamond or other shaped pieces of sheet brass, ⅛ in. thick, and about 1½ in. in length; thus— ; make a small hole at each corner, and a larger hole in the centre; then take about 5 in. of thick brass wire, and bend it at the ends so as to be 4 in. apart, put the ends through the plates; thus— , and solder or get soldered, the wire to the plates underneath; bore holes in the deck 4 in. apart, 2 in. or so forward of the mainmast, and at equal distance from the mid-deck line; fit in the two ends, *a a*, and screw the plates firmly to the deck: if it is desired to be very neat, all the small holes should be countersunk.

Another horse must be made exactly the same way, but 1 in. wider and somewhat stronger, for the mainsheet (diagram, p. 49, *f*), and put as near the edge of the stern as due regard for strength will permit.

The step or socket for the mainmast comes next. Get a short piece of brass tube ⅜ in. internal diameter, and about 7¼ in. long; have a screw soldered into one end; thus—

Bore a hole in the deck exactly amidships, and of exactly the same diameter as the outside of the pipe

How to Make Deck Fittings, Rudder, &c.

or socket 13 in. from the stem, *i. e.* ⅓ the length of the deck; put the brass tube in the hole, and screw it tightly to the bottom of the ship, perpendicular to a line drawn from stem to stern, and also from side to side, so that the mainmast when put in it will be perfectly upright from all sides; file the top of the socket off if too high, so as to leave not more than ¼ in. above the deck.

To make the hatchway or hole (*e* in diagram, p. 49), cut out an oval or oblong hole in the centre of the deck, just abaft or behind the beam (diagram H, p. 39); a water-tight cover or stopper must be made for this with cork, wood, or anything the maker pleases, it matters not provided it is not much above the level of the deck, is water-tight, and can be taken in or out.

Now bore a small hole through the deck, close to the starboard quarter (see *i* in diagram, p. 49); make a short peg to fit it, and call it the *pump;* by inclining the ship towards this hole after sailing, and drawing the peg, you can see if she has leaked, and let the water out if necessary.

The screw-eyes *g g* and *h h*, p. 49, explain themselves by referring to *e, f, h,* and *i,* in diagram, p. 50; they are to hook on the rigging as there shown. These eye-bolts, *h h,* must be as close abaft the mainmast as is consistent with their properly supporting the mainmast, both laterally and aftwards. The reason is that if placed too far aft they would interfere with the mainboom swinging far enough out when running before the wind; the nearer the mainboom is to a right angle with the keel, the steadier and faster the ship will run before the wind. *g g* may be in a line with the horse for the foresheet *c* (diagram, p. 49); care must be taken to screw them through the edge of the deck, and into the gunwale firmly.

To cast the rudder, make a small wooden mould or box similar to that for the keel, about 6 in. long, 3 in. deep, and ½ in. wide.

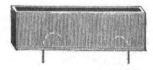

How to Make Deck Fittings, Rudder, &c.

Insert two moderately thick pieces of brass wire through the bottom, and about an inch into the box (as in dotted line), bend them so as to make them stick in the lead, and just as far apart as are the two screw-eyes for this rudder in diagram " stern," p. 44; pour in 1¼ lbs. of melted lead, trim the lead with the rasp, and turn the wires thus— ; and when hooked into the screw-eyes or gudgeons, it should act easily either to right or left. Skilful or tasteful young model yacht sailors can vary the shape of the rudder; I have given the simplest and easiest shape to make.

This completes all the deck fittings necessary for working and sailing the ship, but if on trial the rudder should be too heavy or too light, another must be made —experience is the best guide.

I need hardly say that every direction I have given need not be followed to the letter; those who see and know what is required can do many things in their own way, and much must necessarily be left to individual taste, skill, and ingenuity.

At this stage, varnish the deck with copal varnish, and paint the hull whatever colour or colours fancy dictates; I, however, advise one colour only for the hull, it is less trouble and easier to repaint or repair, eventualities often recurring with model yachts.

CHAPTER IV.

HOW TO FIT MASTS, STANDING AND RUNNING GEAR, &c.

CHAPTER IV.

HOW TO FIT MASTS, STANDING AND RUNNING GEAR, ETC.

THE best material for making masts and spars is bamboo-canes, these require little trimming, can be procured of any thickness and length, and are stronger, lighter, and more elastic than any other kind of wood.

The mainmast must be 38 in. long from the deck, and $\frac{3}{8}$ in. diameter at the foot, to fit the socket or step (diagram, p. 52), slightly tapering to the head or top; the head must be fitted with a brass ferrule or socket for the topmast (like a fishing-rod), and must be *included* in the above 38 in. length, but as the mast has to fit in the step, the depth of the step must be added to it.

If the yacht builder cannot solder or get soldered eyes on the socket at the mast-head, he must lash them on for the foresail, jib, and main and peak halyards, and also for the main backstays; thus—

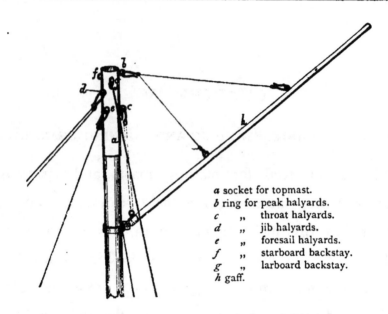

a socket for topmast.
b ring for peak halyards.
c „ throat halyards.
d „ jib halyards.
e „ foresail halyards.
f „ starboard backstay.
g „ larboard backstay.
h gaff.

Rings *d* and *e* must be lashed forward, *b* and *c* aft, *f* and *g* one on each side, *e* and *c* about an inch below *f* and *b*; this is all necessary for the mainmast.

The bowsprit must be 34½ in. long outside the stem and a trifle thicker than the mainmast; be careful to allow the extra length from the stem to the chock (p. 51); it must have rings (these rings can be got at any fishing shop, of all sizes— ○ ○ ○ ○, any size will do, so that the lines used pass easily through)

How to Fit Masts, &c.

for the guys and bobstay lashed on, and hooks for the jib and foresail; tip the end with a band thus, to prevent damage to it by collisions—

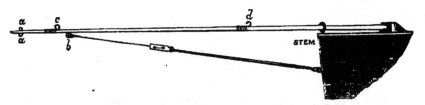

a a rings on each side, close to the end, for the guys.
b ring for bobstay underneath.
c hook for jib tack.   } both to be on top.
d hook for foresail tack. }

The hooks, c and d, for the tacks cannot be lashed on till the sails are made and fitted, for as the jib must always swing clear of the foresail, and the foresail clear of the mainmast, it is best to try them before lashing on these hooks.

These hooks are made of stout brass wire about 1½ in. long, flattened where to be lashed, and the end turned up with the pliers; thus— ; the hook ¼ in. high is plenty, so that the sails may be as low down as possible.

Next, with the pliers make a dozen hooks or so, this

shape and size— ⟨hook⟩, of strong wire; and two of still stouter wire, this shape and size, say 1 in.— ⟨hook⟩; the former are for the various standing and running gear, and the two latter for the foresail sheet and mainsheet. Make also a dozen or so of wood or bone slides to pattern— ⟨slide⟩; one hook and one slide at least is required for every rope that has to be lengthened or shortened. Ladies' bone meshes of suitable width and thickness make the best slides.

The following diagram shows the application and use of these in all instances; say you are fitting the larboard mainbackstay (*f* in diagram, p. 50), make fast your line to the ring (*g*, diagram, p. 60) at the mainmast head, pass the line through two holes of the slide, then through a hook which must be hooked on to the screw-eye (*f*, diagram, p. 50), back through the other hole in the slide, and make it fast there by a knot, only see the line is not too long or too short for convenient working. By this means, as you will soon see, any rope can be fitted that requires it, and can be lengthened or shortened in a moment without danger of slipping; thus—

The best line for all the gear is suitable sizes of fishing-line. If the line kinks, *i.e.* gets into twists, put a yard or so at a time through the loop of the key in a door, cross it over itself once or twice, and rub it backwards and forwards, that takes all the turn out.

The brass wire required may be these sizes—

    ━━━━ for small hooks.
    ▭ „ larger hooks, &c., &c.
    ▭ „ foresheet horse.
    ▭ „ mainsheet horse.

Now comes the mainboom (*d*, diagram, p. 50); it must be 36 in. long, a little thinner than the mainmast, and must be fitted thus—

Put a brass band, *a*, $\frac{1}{2}$ in. wide, round the thicker end, drive a peg strongly into the hollow of the bamboo (the band is to stop it splitting), and screw in a screw-eye, as shown at *b* above; then lash one ring on at *c*, say 15 in. from *a*, and another at *d*, both on the under side of the boom, this last crossways. These two rings are for the mainsheet *f*, and are most important; they must be well put on, the latter, *d*, about 12 in. from the outer end of the boom, so as to work well when the hook *e* is hooked on to the horse for this sheet (viz. mainsheet) at the stern; this hook, *e*, is to be one of the large hooks (as shown p. 62).

In order that the mainsheet should not have to be made too long, and thereby get foul of the stern, &c., when the boom swings over in running or reaching, it is best to have another sheet called the "running sheet," to be fitted as follows:—

Screw a screw-eye (a strong one) into the middle of the deck, just abaft the hatchway, lash a ring to the underside of the mainboom exactly over the screw-eye when the mainboom is amidships, fasten a strong piece of line to the screw-eye, put on a slide, then pass it through a hook, and fasten off to the slide, and hook into the ring on the mainboom; and let this sheet be just so long, that when the mainboom is out as far as it can go for the backstays, it will just take the strain off the backstays, on whichever side it happens to be, in running before the wind.

By means of this running sheet, when the after mainsheet is unhooked, the mainboom can be kept in or let out to any required angle without the sheet fouling, and as the running sheet is fast to the ship only, it can be easily unhooked from the mainboom when unrigging. Still, this running sheet is not absolutely necessary, but is a very great convenience.

To attach the mainboom to the mast, and allow it to move freely, get a strip of sheet brass ⅜ in. wide, just long enough to go *round the mast* (close to the deck), and ⅜ in. over at each end; bore a hole at each end thus— ●●●●●●●●● , and bend it round the mast. With the pincers nip the two ends close together, and so that the two holes are in a line thus—

Now put the screw-eye at the end of the mainboom between these two holes, fasten it there with a bit of wire turned round at each end; thus—

No arrangement can be more perfect or stronger than this.

The above operation has to be repeated for the *jaws* or inner end of the gaff (*c* in diagram, p. 50), but the ring must fit the head of the mast instead of the foot.

The gaff must be 21½ in. long, and a little thinner than the mainboom; thus—

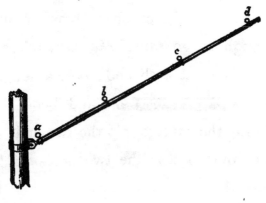

Lash one large ring at *a*, as close to the end as possible, two others, smaller, further out at *b* and *c*, and one at *d*; all these rings must be on the top side of the gaff, *d* an inch from the outer end of the gaff, for the sheet of the topsail to be hooked on (see frontispiece).

The topmast is a taper bamboo, the lower end of which must fit tightly into the socket at the mainmast head, it must be 24 in. long outside the socket; lash two small rings at opposite sides, ½ in. from the head, put a knob on the top (called the truck), and the topmast is ready.

The boom for the foresail (*i. e.* the spar that extends the foot of the sail) must be 20 in. long, that for the jib 25½ in. long, and both about the thickness of the gaff; here, however, use your judgment. Lash rings on for the sheets of each; each must have a sliding sheet (see drawing at end of this chapter) the same as for the mainsheet (p. 63); the jib sheet, however, requires no hook at the end, but must be made fast to the bowsprit, or, if greater precision is required, a horse may be made for the jib as for the other sails, and fastened in its

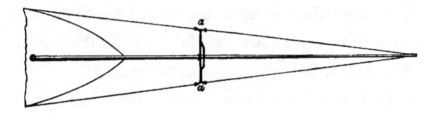

proper place across the bowsprit, and to the guys as above; it may be made of thin brass wire, as follows, merely taking care that it is the right length, and that the horse is an inch or so less than the foresheet horse. It is made of four pieces of wire, the horse bent, as in diagram below, and the other pieces soldered to it; the

guys may be passed through the loops *a* on their respective sides, and knots made to keep them in place; it will be perfectly self-acting, and never get out of place; the weather guy being always tight will always keep it nearly horizontal; it makes the jib, like the other sails, a good *driving* as well as steering sail. Besides the above rings, another must be lashed on the outer end (all the rings on the boom are underneath) of each boom, *a* and *b*, about 2½ in. from the end; thus—

and must both be crosswise, as they are to secure these booms to their respective hooks (see *c* and *d* on bowsprit, p. 61; and also diagram, p. 70). This manner of fixing these sails is the best to keep them tight and flat when in use.

This diagram shows the best mode of fixing the tacks of jib and foresail to the bowsprit; by this means, when the sail fills with the wind, it raises the after end of the boom, *depresses the fore end*, and thus tightens the luff of the sail and keeps it taut, which is very necessary. This diagram also shows how the jib and foresail swing clear of each other; also that the jib must not quite go to the end of the bowsprit, or it may be knocked off.

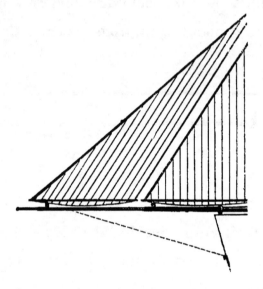

When all the rings are carefully and neatly lashed on, say with strong white thread,—lashing is the best, because it does not weaken the spars by making it necessary to bore holes in them,—varnish all the lashings with copal varnish, it will preserve them and prevent them slipping.

Each maker must use a little judgment, and *under-*

stand what he is going to do before he does it, and as in some instances the spars, or what not, may be a little too long, the best plan is for the maker to try each and everything before spoiling his work.

Enlarged Diagram of how to fix the sliding sheets for the respective booms, i. e. jib, fore, and main.

CHAPTER V.

HOW TO MAKE THE SAILS AND SET THEM.

CHAPTER V.

HOW TO MAKE THE SAILS AND SET THEM.

THE speed and precision in the sailing of a model yacht, depend much more upon the sails than the hull, and the greatest care must be taken in making them.

If pains are taken to carry out the following directions, an excellent suit of self-acting sails will be the result.

The best material is either bleached or unbleached calico, 1 yd. wide, at 8*d*. per yd., and for a 2-ft. yacht 10*d*. per yd.; 3 yds. are sufficient for a 3-ft. boat. Steep the calico in clean water, and dry it across a line before using it. It is always better to cut the patterns of the sails out in paper, and try them in their places, before cutting the stuff.

On the next page are given diagrams of the four sails for a cutter, and as all are cut on the cross, care must be taken when hemming them not to pucker or stretch the material; the after leach, *i.e.* the behind edge of all the sails, must be the selvedge, and must not be hemmed. In cutting out, allowance must be made for the hems, the measurements given being the actual sizes required.

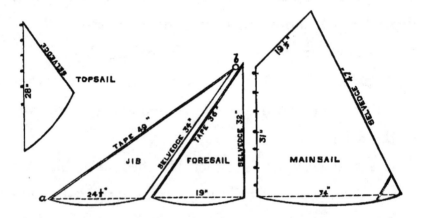

The bottoms of the sails must be slightly rounded, as shown above, and a narrow tape must be sewn across, as shown by the dotted lines, to keep the sails from stretching.

All the sewing for these sails can be done perfectly and expeditiously with any lock-stitch machine; it will sew them exactly even without puckering, and all that has to be done by hand is to fasten off the corners. I make all my own sails, and can, without hurry, make a full large suit for a 3-ft. boat in an evening.

The selvedges are not to be hemmed, because the after leaches of all the sails should allow the wind to pass freely off. The sizes of the sails are marked on the diagrams distinctly; allow ⅛ in. extra on the outer leach of the mainsail, from *c* to *d* in diagram below, so that it may be slightly loose; this helps to steer materially, as the leach will shake before the body of the sail, if the vessel comes too much up in the wind, and so losing its power allow the ship to fall off and sail steadily. This diagram shows how to cut the head of the mainsail; the dotted line shows how the sail would be if cut straight, therefore cut straight from *a* to *b*, then slant 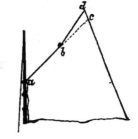 off to *d* at rather more than midway from *a* to *c*. Make eight or ten eyelet holes at equal distances in the hoist of the mainsail, and fix a ring or grummet of twine in each hole to fit loosely round the mainmast; these are better than brass rings or wooden hoops, and weigh nothing.

The lower outer corner of the mainsail should be double for 2 or 3 in. (see diagram, p. 76), to strengthen it; in fact, the corners of all the sails are none the worse for being so doubled.

Now fix the sail to the mainboom and gaff; with a needle and strong thread is best: do not pull the sail too tight. The boom will then be 2 in. or so too long; do not cut that off, it is useful to turn the ship with; leave also the extra length of the gaff, it looks better. The head of the sail must be laced or tied to the gaff at intervals of 1 in., but on no account lace the foot of the sails to the booms; (for reason why see p. 29) the sail is then ready.

In setting, *i.e.* putting on, the mainsail, when you have passed the foot of the mainmast through the jaws of the gaff and all the grummets, then before passing it through the jaws of the mainboom, put on an India-rubber ring, and then the mainboom; the ring must be pretty tight to the mast, and is very useful to keep the mainboom from slipping up. For position of this ring, see *k* in diagram, p. 50.

To hold the mainsail up, the inner ring on the gaff and lower after-ring on the mainmast head, must have stout twine passed through and made fast. This is called the throat-halyards.

The gaff must be kept at its proper angle by means of twine made fast to the next ring on the gaff, passed through a hook, which hook into the upper after-ring at the mainmast head, and fasten off at the third ring on the gaff. This is called the peak-halyards. With these two, peak and throat-halyards, you can easily fix the mainsail, so that when the mainboom *is half an inch above the deck at the mast*, and about an inch or so clear of the mainsheet horse at the stern, the sail shall set perfectly flat.

The annexed arrangement of the topmast stay is excellent; it keeps tight the luff of the jib, slightly slacks up the after-leach, and is no trouble whatever to fix or unfix. It simply consists of putting a large ring (so that the hook can pass through) at the top point of the jib, pass the topmast stay-hook through, and hook it into a ring sewn on to the luff any distance down you think sufficient, as in diagram at side. *a* topmast, *b* topmast stay, *c* mainsail, *d* jib.

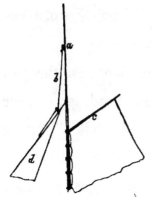

The jib must have a piece of tape stitched from *a* to *b* on the double, ½ in. each side (see p. 76), and a ring sewn on at *b*. A hem only in the luff would be useless on account of the strain. The same must be done to the foresail; hem the bottoms, and leave the selvedges as they are.

Lash them to their respective yards or booms (see diagram, pp. 69 and 70). Of course the sail must be on the top of the boom, and the rings and sheets underneath; try them in their places; now lash on the hooks to the bowsprit (see p. 61), and you will see exactly where to put them; mind, the jib must swing just clear of both bowsprit and foresail (see frontispiece), and the foresail just clear of the mast and stem. Fit both these sails at the head with a hook and slide, the end of the line to be fast to the head of the sail, and the hook is to hook into the rings (respectively) at the mainmast head (see frontispiece), which shows exactly how all the sails set. The booms for these sails (jib and foresail) must be cut close, as there is no room to spare.

The topsail is 28 in. high, and reaches from the large ring in the jaws of the gaff (*a*, p. 66) to the topmast head, and before cutting it out the mainsail must be tried and set. The shape of this sail depends on the peak or angle of the gaff; and having made a pattern in paper to fit thus, make eyelet holes equidistant from *b* to head of the mainmast, and put in rings of twine to fit the topmast loosely, as was done before with mainsail; fasten a hook to each of the corners, *a*,

F

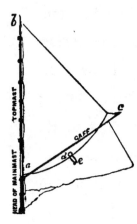

b, c, to hook into the respective rings already placed for them;—if the hooks are too short, use a piece of twine sewn to the sail, at *b* and *c* only, to lengthen them;—now sew a button at the edge of the curved bottom of the sail at *d*, and a loop to button on it on the head of the mainsail at *e*; this keeps the rounded foot always flat.

The masts, sails, and gear being now all complete, try them on, and make any little alterations that may be necessary. If my directions have been intelligently followed, the sails will be exactly the sizes and shape of those in the lateral diagram, frontispiece.

A strong, fine piece of line, fitted with a slide and hook, in the usual way, the end made fast to the topmast head ring forward, and the hook to be hooked into the ring at the jib head or top corner (see the diagram p. 80, and also frontispiece). This is to raise the foot of the jib, if required, and also to steady the topmast;

this is a simple though not so effectual a topmast stay as that given, p. 80.

The sails must be as tight and flat as possible when set, and the mast must be kept exactly upright by the backstays aft, and by the jib and foresail forward, the tape on the jib and foresail taking the place of stays or ropes used for that purpose in ordinary yachts, which are by this means dispensed with in models.

Sail and mast-making is not yet done. Another suit of masts, spars, and sails, of exactly two-thirds the length, breadth, and height of these, must be made. It is called the *storm suit*, and is used when the wind is too strong for the first suit. Reefing is not practicable in a cutter.

Some model yachtsmen have three or four suits of sails, &c.; I find two sufficient, because I don't sail a yacht when there is scarcely a breath, and I don't sail one when it blows a hurricane, and so I find two suits enough. Still if you race in matches, and mean winning, you must have both a larger and smaller suit, for you can never tell what the wind will be on the race day, and must be prepared.

Now that all your sails are complete, paint the hull, and varnish the deck again; tip the end of the masts and booms the colour of your yacht, it looks ship-shape.

A pole of pine or deal, 6 ft. long, with a double hook at one end, is required to handle and turn the ship. Herewith drawing of the hook. One side is to push the ship out, and the other to pull it in or turn it.

Lastly, two bags are needed, each to contain 1 lb. of shot, for shifting ballast to trim the ship, if you require her deeper aft or forward.

CHAPTER VI.

HOW TO SAIL AND STEER A MODEL YACHT.

CHAPTER VI.

HOW TO SAIL AND STEER A MODEL YACHT.

THE action of the wind upon the sails of a vessel presses her down sideways and forwards, this causes the lee bow (viz. that on the side opposed to the wind) to be more immersed than the weather bow (or wind side bow), and the curve of the bow acting like a rudder or wedge, forces the vessel strongly up in the wind, in exact proportion to the strength of the wind. This is a simple mechanical law any one can understand after watching a model yacht for five minutes, and to counteract while utilizing it, I build a model yacht much deeper aft than forward, make the bowsprit very long, the jib and foresail large, and the mainsail narrow at the head and slack in the outer leach or edge. These arrangements, properly adjusted, nearly neutralize this tendency of the lee bow to force the ship to windward, and leave only just enough, so that by setting the sails in the way shown later, a model yacht steers itself perfectly. Great care must be taken not to overdo it, otherwise the vessel will run off the wind, and not steer herself at all.

The part which the increased depth of keel aft plays in steering a model yacht is this; as the sails are very evenly balanced, and exert little more force at the stern than at the bow when *the vessel is upright in the water;* yet even then there is always the tendency more or less to come up in the wind, and as the bow is not so deep as the stern, the lateral pressure of all the sails forces the vessel sideways (called leeway),— she makes more *leeway forward than aft*, and thus this particular arrangement helps to make her steer herself. Necessarily, when the wind blows strongly it is of very great use, and enables increased length of bowsprit to be dispensed with : too long a bowsprit is a great drawback, it dips in the water, and is difficult to fasten firmly.

Again, a model vessel being well up by the stem, and deep aft, possesses another power of self-steering, viz. when the wind presses her down forward (when on the wind), it lightens her aft; this, of course, permits her to gripe more to windward, as she holds more water forward and less aft, but if she comes up too much, so as to relieve the mainsail of a great part of its pressure, the opposite action results, the bow is lightened and the stern depressed exactly in proportion, so that under all circumstances the vessel possesses a self-acting power to steer herself.

Now, as just shown, a model yacht, partly by the action of the sails (particularly the mainsail), and partly by the action of the lee bow, will always keep close to the wind,—in fact, too close; therefore, to make her steer herself, the jib and foresail are kept in a little closer (*i. e.* more in a parallel line with the keel) than the mainsail. So if the vessel comes too close to the wind, first the outer leach of the mainsail loses its power and shakes, and if this does not suffice, *as it should*, to make her fall off again, the whole mainsail will shake, and as the jib and foresail must keep full, the ship pays off till the mainsail fills again. So an equilibrium is attained, and in a steady wind, on the sea for instance, the yacht would sail on in the same direction as if on rails, till the sails dropped in pieces.

This diagram gives the disposition of the booms by means of their respective sheets. To make a yacht sail full and by, *i.e.* close to the wind, and neither run off or shake, the jib is nearly parallel to the bowsprit, the foresail less so, and the mainsail least

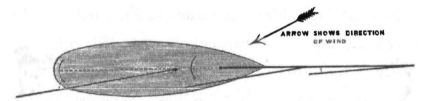

of all, and clearly shows the principle, for it is evident that if the vessel turned more towards the wind, the mainsail would shake, and the jib and foresail keeping still full, would turn the ship back to her course again, viz. "full and by." On the other hand, she cannot run off the wind, because the mainsail, well full as it must be, if she ran off, would bring her up again instantly.

I presume every intelligent person understands that a vessel cannot sail with her head to the wind (all the sails must shake, and she would go a-stern), and few vessels can sail nearer, if so near, as at an angle of 45° to the wind. In the next diagram (p. 92), will be shown the way to sail the vessel in any *possible* direction, and how the booms must be disposed, and the rudder or rudders and ballast bags used to accomplish it.

The wind is supposed to be blowing in the direction the arrow flies, and by holding this diagram with the arrow towards the point the wind is blowing from, your vessel can be made to sail in every direction there indicated.

No vessel can head nearer towards the wind shown by the arrow, than *a* and *aa*, one being on the larboard, the other on the starboard tack (as it is called), *i.e.* about 45°, four points of a compass, or half a right angle.

92   *Model Yachts and Model Yacht Sailing.*

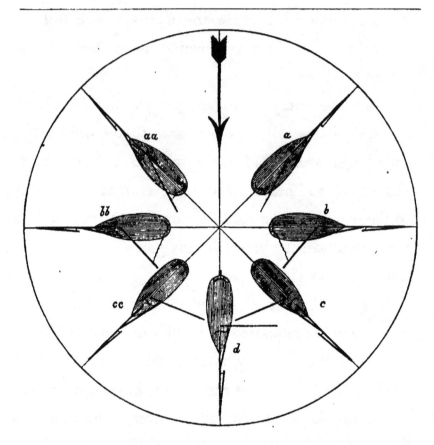

The vessel at *a* is therefore sailing close to the wind on the larboard tack, with the sails disposed for that purpose, as already shown (p. 90); to put her on the other tack, simply turn her in the direction *aa*, head to wind; the sails, being self-acting, will go over of themselves by the force of the wind, and she will continue on that tack till stopped or turned.

To sail her as at *b*, ease off the mainsheet till the mainboom is at an angle of 45° (this is called wind abeam) to the keel of the ship, and she will do so.; it is seldom necessary to touch the jib or foresheets, leave those sails as at *a*. To sail her as at *bb*, turn her round, head to wind, and the sails take the same place on the other side, and that is done.

To sail as at *c*, let go the mainsheet altogether; if the wind is not too strong, she will do so, but if it is too strong, a light rudder, self-acting, of about $\frac{1}{4}$ lb. weight must be made and used, and that will do it. Turn her round as before, head to wind, if you wish to sail her as at *cc*. The rule is simple enough: if the sails are set, and propel her in a given direction on the one tack, she will, if turned, sail in the corresponding direction on the other tack.

To run before the wind at *d*, with the mainsheet let go, hook on the heavy rudder, and she will run more or less true before the wind, according to the perfection with which the ship is built and the rudder balanced. The cause is this: if the vessel turns, say to starboard, the wind necessarily presses her over to larboard, the self-acting rudder (being exactly upright when the ship is upright) falls over to larboard also, and instantly puts her straight again; the exact opposite takes place should she turn to larboard, and so *she must sail straight before the wind.*

When the wind is very light, it will sometimes occur, that the vessel on account of the large jib and foresail, will run off the wind; if so, put one or two of the bags of shot inside in her bows, and most likely that will remedy it; if not, change the angles of the jib and foresails, *i.e.* let the jib sheet out more, and haul the foresheet in as much as the jib was, so that you would then be steering more by the foresail than by the jib. This is sure to succeed.

Before all these manœuvres can be successfully performed, some little practice is necessary, of course;

ships, like everything else, have little ways of their own, and must be studied.

The topsail must always be kept set, and needs no touching after being once set, for though of no great use as a propelling sail, save off the wind, it is so as a steadying sail, being so lofty. My experience has taught me never to dispense with it.

To prove the certainty with which a model yacht must sail in the direction intended, you can, as an experiment, put the vessel's head in the water in any direction you please, and she will immediately take the *course for which the sails are set*, no matter how you put her in the water. For instance, place her in the water, *head to wind*, with the mainsheet let go, and the heavy rudder on, *i.e.* to sail as at *d* (p. 92), and she will of her own account turn round and run before the wind, an operation which, to those not in the secret, seems like magic.

Rigged in the way I have described, with every part of the standing and running rigging being made fast by hooks and slides, a cutter can be completely unrigged in one minute, and rigged again in three minutes: I have done it in these times easily. This is a very great advantage; there are no knots to make, no time is lost, and yet the rigging is as strong and as perfect as possible, and never fails till worn out.

I hope I have now made all clear, and that my readers may be enabled to build ships, and rig them to sail with as much satisfaction to themselves as mine are to me.

Model yachts can be rigged to sail and steer well, as schooners, luggers, &c., and I have vessels rigged in those ways. Should this treatise meet with success, I purpose writing a second, dealing with this subject.

MATERIALS FOR MODEL SHIPS.

BLOCK of wood: white pine or soft deal; at almost any wood-yard, and particularly at those in the neighbourhood of the docks; cost for a 2-ft. boat, 2s. 6d., for a 3-ft., about 10s.

Masts, booms, &c., of bamboo canes, at florists, who sell cheap bamboos for about 8d. per dozen for gardening purposes; the best can be selected, and they will serve for masts, all the spars of a 2-ft. boat, and for booms, gaffs, and topmasts of 3-ft. boats. Bamboos for the mast, bowsprit, and mainboom of 3-ft. boats can be got at fishing-tackle shops and toy shops; both sell cheap bamboo fishing-rods at about 3d. each. They can be easily selected of the required thickness and length. Excellent bamboo canes for booms, gaffs, and topmasts can also be obtained at umbrella shops and stick shops, but they cost more—1*d.*, 2*d.*, or 3*d.*, and even 6*d.* each.

Twine, white line, &c., for standing and running rigging, can be had at fishing-tackle or cord and twine shops.

Calico and tape at any linendrapers.

Lead at any plumber's shop, 2*d.* or 3*d.* per lb.

Paint and copal at any oilman's. Paint 6*d* or 8*d.* per lb. Copal varnish about 1*s.* per pint; 3*d.* worth is enough for a 3-ft. boat.

Brass and copper wire at most ironmongers, as also screw-eyes of any size. If the two former cannot be readily obtained, Messrs. Jackson and Sons, 17, Sun Street, Finsbury, keep every size in brass and copper wire, and every thickness in brass and copper sheets; all these are sold by weight.

All sizes of rings can be had at fishing-tackle shops. 1*d* or 2*d.* per dozen.

Ferrules or bands for tipping the ends of spars to prevent them splitting, can be got at fishing-tackle

Materials for Model Ships. 99

shops, and the amateur builder can file off any length required; they are very cheap. For small bands, pipe mounts are excellent, very light and thin, and easily cut to any length. Most tobacconists keep them in all sizes, 1*d* or 2*d*. each.

If the boat builder cannot get or make bands, lash or bind the ends of the spars neatly and strongly with good white thread, and then paint it well with copal. It will answer every purpose, but does not look so neat and trim.

Lastly, slides can be made of any hard wood as well as of bone, and the requisite holes bored with a bradawl, and then seared with a red-hot skewer.

GLOSSARY.

ABAFT, } towards the stern.
AFT,
AMIDSHIPS, middle of a ship or anything.
BACKSTAY, ropes which support the mast sideways and backwards.
BEAM, breadth of a vessel, also the support of the deck.
BOARD, the distance sailed on one tack.
BOBSTAY, the rope that keeps the bowsprit down; reaches from end of bowsprit to cutwater.
BOOM, any spar used to extend the foot of a sail.
BOW, front part of a vessel.
BOWSPRIT, spar projecting in front of a vessel to set the jibs on.
BULWARKS, the wooden railings round the deck of a ship.
CHOCK, piece of wood to hold anything firmly.
CLOSE, a vessel being as near the direction of the wind as she can go without shaking.
COUNTER, the projection of the stern.
CUTWATER, the sharp part of the bow.
DECK, the covering of the ship to keep the water out, &c.
DRAW, a ship draws so much water, *i. e.* it is so many feet in the water.
ENTRANCE, the forward part of the bottom of a vessel, tapered off to the cutwater, so as to cleave the water.
FALL OFF, when a vessel turns from the direction of the wind.

FOOT, bottom of a mast or sail.
FORE AND AFT, any sail which does not cross the mast.
FORESAIL, sail in forepart of a ship.
FORWARD, fore part of a ship.
FULL, when the sails are distended by the wind.
FULL AND BY, close to the wind yet not shaking. *See* CLOSE.
GAFF, the spar which supports the head of a fore and aft sail.
GRUMMET, a ring made of rope.
GUDGEON, a sort of eye-bolt for the rudder to work on.
GUNWALE, top of the side of a ship on which the deck is fastened.
GUY, rope to keep and secure the bowsprit, &c., laterally.
HALYARDS, ropes used to hoist the sails.
HATCHWAY, openings in the deck of a ship.
HEAD, top of a mast or sail.
HOIST, height a sail is pulled up.
HOLD, the inside of a ship.
HORSE, long bars of iron on which the sheets of sails work.
HULL, body of a ship.
JAWS, any arrangement to secure a gaff or boom to a mast, and allow it to swing from side to side, &c.
JIB, a three-cornered sail in front of a ship.
KEEL, the centre of the bottom of a ship.
LACED, tied in a certain way.
LARBOARD, left.
LEACH, edge of a sail, generally the side.

Glossary

LEE, side of a vessel farthest from that from which the wind blows.

LEE-WAY, the side-way motion of a ship caused by the side pressure of the wind.

LUFF, to go closer to the wind.

LUFF (of a sail), edge of a sail nearest the wind.

MAIN-HALYARDS, ropes to hoist the mainsail.

MAINMAST, the lower mast in a cutter.

MAINSHEET, the rope or gear to secure and regulate the after lower corner of the mainsail.

NEAR, same as close. *See* CLOSE.

OFF. *See* FALL OFF.

OVERALL, from stem to stern.

PAY OFF. *See* FALL OFF.

PEAK, the angular head of the mainsail.

PEAK-HALYARDS, ropes to hoist the outer end of the gaff.

QUARTERS, both sides of a ship close to the stern.

REACHING, sailing with the wind abeam or nearly so.

REEFING, reducing the sails by tying them up smaller.

RUN, the after part of the bottom of a vessel, tapered off to the stern-post, so as to leave the water freely.

RUNNING, sailing with the wind astern or nearly so.

RUNNING GEAR, any ropes used for hoisting the sails or yards.

SELVEDGE, the even edge of linen, canvas, &c.

SHAKE, when the sails shake in the wind and so lose their power.

SHEER, slope of a vessel downwards to midships from stem and stern.

SHEET, robes used to secure and regulate lower after corner of sails.

STANDING GEAR, any fixed ropes, as backstays, &c.

STARBOARD, right side.

STAY, ropes used to support the masts forward only.

STEM. *See* CUTWATER.

STEP, socket for heel of mast, &c.

STERN, the after part of a vessel.

STERN-POST, end of keel and run, upon which the rudder is fixed.

TACK, forward lower corner of a sail.

TACK, to make a zigzag course so as to get to windward.

TAUT, tight.

TOPMAST, the second mast from the deck.

WATERLINE, line of the water on the side, &c., of a ship, showing how deep she is in the water.

WEATHER, side of a vessel, &c., nearest the wind.

WINDWARD, in direction of the wind, the side from which the wind blows.

CONTESTS ON THE OPEN SEA BETWEEN CUTTERS "GOLDEN CREST" AND "STORM ALONG."

1st Trial. Strong breeze, rough sea, storm sails, foot of sails laced to booms; $1\frac{1}{4}$ miles on each tack. "Storm Along" beat on each tack, about 50 yds. to windward.

2nd Trial. Large suits, light breeze and sea; $1\frac{1}{2}$ miles on each tack. "Storm Along," all sails laced to booms; "Golden Crest," mainsail free and jib laced. "Storm Along" led a few yards once; "Golden Crest" beat, 20 yds. in 2 boards.

3rd Trial. Sails as in 2nd Trial, moderate breeze and sea; 2 boards, $1\frac{1}{4}$ miles each. "Golden Crest" beat, 20 yds. on each.

4th Trial. Sails as above, moderate breeze and sea, *interchanged sails.* "Storm Along" beat, $\frac{1}{4}$ mile on each tack of 1 mile length each.

5th Trial. Moderate breeze and sea, "Storm Along" own sails all free from booms, and "Golden Crest" all laced; 2 boards of 1 mile each. "Storm Along" beat, $\frac{1}{4}$ mile to windward. 1 last board of 1 mile; "Golden Crest," all sails free from booms, *i.e.* both vessels own sails and alike. "Storm Along" beat, $\frac{1}{4}$ mile dead to windward.

6th Trial. Gentle breeze and sea, full suits and each their own. "Storm Along" beat, 40 yds. to windward in $\frac{1}{2}$ mile board. "Golden Crest" headreached a little, this wind and sea showing her best points.

TIME TABLE OF TWO MODEL YACHT REGATTAS.

4-ft. cutters. Wind strong, E. by S. 4 vessels in each heat. Course once up and down pond, 259 yds. long, 30 yds. wide; length of pond being E. and W.

	Start.		Run.		Beat back.		Time.
	H.	M.	H.	M.	H.	M.	M.
1st Heat	4	14	4	16¾	4	23½	9½
2nd „	4	33	4	36	4	42¾	9¾
3rd „	4	50	4	53	4	59	9
Loser's Heat . . .	5	4	5	7	5	14¼	10¼
Final „ . . .	5	20	5	23½	5	31	11

In this race, final heat, the three first winners fouled, and the winner of loser's heat won.

3-ft. cutters. Wind strong, W. by S. Course as above.

	Start.			Run.			Beat back.			Time.	
	H.	M.	S.	H.	M.	S.	H.	M.	S.	M.	S.
1st Heat	5	14	50	5	18	30	5	26	23	11	33
2nd „	5	35	30	5	39	8	5	46	40	11	10
3rd „	6	3	5	6	6	40	6	16	5	13	0
Loser's Heat . . .	6	23	5	6	26	30	6	36	10	13	5
Final „ . . .	6	43	52	6	47	25	6	54	50	10	58

This last race won by 6 in. only.

By examining above table, it appears to novices almost incredible that such precision can be attained in model yacht sailing. All the heats were won by a few feet only, and some by inches.

BEST WATERS FOR SAILING MODEL YACHTS.

The best ponds for sailing model yachts in London are: (1) Victoria Park Pond, but only when the wind is E. or W. (2) Round Pond, Kensington, in any winds, all sides of this pond being clear of trees. (3) Serpentine, in any wind.

Hampstead and Highgate ponds are also available, but have muddy edges, and seldom a true wind on account of the high banks.

There are also good ponds on Clapham Common and Peckham Rye.

on
—3-35

CPSIA information can be obtained
at www.ICGtesting.com
Printed in the USA
LVHW081745060219
606612LV00011B/295/P